R.I.P.
Poetry Collection

R.I.P.
Poetry Collection
REFLECTIONS, ILLUMINATIONS, PERCEPTIONS

SCOTT ANTHONY

authorHOUSE®

AuthorHouse™
1663 Liberty Drive
Bloomington, IN 47403
www.authorhouse.com
Phone: 1-800-839-8640

Published by AuthorHouse   10/01/2012

ISBN: 978-1-4772-7565-8 (sc)
ISBN: 978-1-4772-7564-1 (hc)
ISBN: 978-1-4772-7566-5 (e)

Library of Congress Control Number: 2012918233

Contents

Reflections

Illuminations

Perceptions

Dedicated to Gale Guidry and Roann Romero & in Rememberance to all that has been affected from cancer or serious illnesses.

God bless those, we are all connected.

A light

Live a life of action and be a light.
Forgive the over reactions, they just
see a spotlight. Make matters work
not worse. You are worth the goodness
you give to the sick and the hurt.
Listen and learn from the many concerned.
The wisdom of one can make the wrong
take a turn. So, as long as you feel the
burn, keep it real, and you will always
yearn. That's right, I was told give it your
all and it will return to you ten fold.
Forget the over reactions, they just see a
spotlight. The elements of life can reach
many heights, but it's up to you to be
a light.

A moment

In a moment, you will be seeing me.
In a moment, you will be leaving me.
In a moment, you will believe in me.
In a moment, you will be free of me.
All it takes is a moment, a glance,
a chance, a dance, a moment.

Beams of shining delight

Behind my cluttered thoughts, I shutter a fine thought. I'm done with the fights I fought. It's time to see the feelings inside me, feel them rising, and release those beams of shining delight. Around the circles in my head, I cover myself as I lie in my bed to rest because I did my best like I said. It's no surprise that I healed up right. I feel my life is bright, whether I am awake or I am asleep throughout the day or the night. I will release those beams of shining delight.

Blessed

You and I are blessed to rise every
day, to abreast the sun's light, and
to rest, like the sun sets, for the
night.
You and I are blessed to survive
every day, to try the hands of
time, and to test, like the sun rises,
for the best.
Where, when, why? Because
You and I are blessed.

Canvas of art

With God's paintbrush of wonder, every
Heavenly touch, every unearthly stroke,
shows us.
Our heart, bright red with trust.
Our soul, light yellow ready for us.
Our mind, real dark pink to think so
much color is in all of us. All along the
sea of bright blue hues, also among the
white light beaming onto our canvas
of art.
With God's paintbrush of wonder, every
Heavenly touch, every unearthly stroke,
shows us.
Our love that flows deep amber.
Our smile that glows sweet where ever.
Our thoughts as they grow green when ever
we know so much color is in all of us. All
along the biggest star burning bright onto
our canvas of art.
With God's paintbrush of wonder, every
Heavenly touch, every unearthly stroke,
shows us. We are a canvas of art.

Endless inspirations

*Bad situations happen, but it's how you react
to them. Can you forgive your friend? Can
you live out your plans? Can you get the
messages that are sent? It may take dedication,
some might say many connections, but it's
just days in a maze of endless inspirations.
In the beginning, the reasons are on lost land,
within the penmanship life is a trip, and you
get tossed from hand to hand. Then it's really
and truly up to you to understand and
comprehend. It may take admiration, some
might say many directions, but it's just days
in a maze of endless inspirations.*

Especially among the stormy seas

So far away with the moonlight shining it's pale beauty, while the North Star guides you and me along the night. As we sail, we may prevail or fail along the seven seas, but know once we cast on, we will pass on good fortune and good deeds. From cruising the coast to coasting speeds, especially among the stormy seas. So close always with the sunlight beaming its rays, while that huge golden star seems to lead you and me throughout the days. As we sail through the motions we weather within the oceans, we can't loose sight from what might harm the devotion we live and breathe. From the deep emotions to emotional sickness, especially among the stormy seas.

Forbidden fruit

If you work for the truth, you will find your forbidden fruit. It's how you use your God given talents through life's challenges. There's no need to fear it, so get into the spirit. The materialistic will shed it's need for greed, unrealistic schemes, and empty dreams. There's your door, so open up those opportunistic goals to show you have a place of your own, you have transportation to stay or go, and your abilities are worth so much more than you give yourself credit for. If you work for the truth, you will find your forbidden fruit.

Freedom is born

Hell, I'm not a mind reader, but I can read people well. I spell L.O.V.E., I hope you can read it loud and clear, and you feel your heart swell. No need to be scorned or torn anymore because beyond the thorns there's redemption, and that's where freedom is born. I can tell when you are feeling tired, wired up, fired up, when enough is enough and you're fed up. So what's up, forget being burned up from the great loss that turned up. No need to be scorned or torn anymore because beyond the thorns there's redemption, and that's where freedom is born.

From the salt of the Earth

*As the World turns in the nightlight of the
moon, there shines a birth from the salt of
the Earth, that's me, so free.
As the diamond mines become greater
than me, it also showed the costly times
became richer than the free. However,
together, the free and me fought to
survive a birth from the salt of the Earth.
As the World burns in the sunlight of
the noon, there shines our worth from
the salt of the Earth, helps us to be seen.
As the fault lines shown deeper than me,
it also showed the broken skies grown
bigger than the sea. However, together,
the sea and me sought to find our worth
from the salt of the Earth.*

Hairy situation

Life is beauty, the ocean air is
breath taking, the open fields
are so overwhelming to me. That
is what makes it so hard to see
the fences. You surround yourself
with steel and your words never
seem real. What a hairy situation,
it feels like I need an invitation
to be in your presence.
Life is amazing, the skies are
opened wide, the birds fly in
groups from side to side. We hold
hands, compromise, and take a
stand. You put your best foot
forward to lay down the fences
and to make amends to all our
messes.
Life is beautifully amazing that
is no debating. You realize what
is around us and forget all the
bad stuff because that doesn't
last, but the nature is vast and
expels a wonderland to a
hairy situation.

Have faith and believe

Have faith and believe, then the stress will subside, so you can release from within and live a life. Don't hold it in, if you do, how can you mend? Don't pretend, life is too short, but it's not the end. If you judge, it's your fault that you never had or became a never was. Life is a puzzle, simply put it together. Don't believe you have it worst, believe you can have it better. Forget the superstitions, there aren't any curses. Open a book for knowledge because your mind is thirsting. Vote, it's your opinion. Don't provoke, it's not your decision. Only react to the facts under any condition. If you read what I write, you might not see my truth, but if you have a feeling or emotion, then that's what I wanted to do for you. People loose or become lost every day. Choose to put up a welcome home sign in their way. One smile along many miles can brighten any ones day. Don't say you really want or really need, just pray for your wants and those needs, then have faith and believe.

Homesick

I have painted my fears red, so they
are covered up with a touch of love
from all those hectic homesick years.
However, if my house could talk, the
walls would say, we lived in the calm
of each day. The shake up of squalls
left us to worry through the stormy
weather, but the support beams kept
it all together. I have painted my
tears yellow, so they are made up of
a golden touch like a halo from all
those hectic homesick years. It seems
my greatest room does rest in the
living room's space, no matter my
situations, no matter my conditions,
this foundation has the best intentions
of grace. I am not a painter with brush
or stick, but I am the colors that can
brush a touch to the homesick.

I am a book

I am a book, I am a novel to inspire
at best, I am the chapters that transpire
into text, and I am the pages that breath
fire to what comes next and so it
should. I am a book, I am the passion so
heart felt and so well put, I am the ink
and the pen held together to do the
rhyme and the reason like I knew they
could, and I am the words of expression
shared because of the caring trees that
helped to branch out life's ideas from
flatten pieces of wood. I am a book, I
am in a bind, but I don't mind because
this collection is one of a kind, I am
line after line a great connection to
an open mind, I am a gift, a vision, a
sign to design a tell all account of
life's deepest thoughts, untold emotions,
and distant feelings, I am someone else's
words that insist an opinion on my World's
greatest novel like I knew they would, I
am a book.

I am a heart

I am a heart; I am a field of dreams being cultivated
So along the beaten paths I start, I am the growth from
Caring ways that are off the charts, and I am a softer
Side among the harder days so next time remember
There is a better part. I am a heart; I am a permanent
Mark of hope, trust, and love that is sent to save like
Noah's Ark, I am a shelter, a home, and a fire burning
Bright to give a light on life from the dark, and I am
Joined from a heart of love and the blood that flows
Life into the womb then depart to become one soul
To cherish a birthmark. I am a heart; I am shared in
A conversation that is heart to heart, I am fair in a
Situation toward someone's broken heart, I am
Prepared to mention deep feelings are at heart, I am
Really there in times of need taken to heart, I am
A heart.

I am a mind

I am a mind, I am the peace within
a piece of mind that is a part of
mankind, I am always spinning
those wheels that keep the thoughts
cruising by, and I am a brainstorm
of ideas waiting to be placed not
erased because that's when the best
inspiration is made so defined. I am
a mind, I am scatterbrain when a
million and one things weigh all at
once and puts a bind, I am connected
to every part of the body balancing
the actions and the reactions to find
satisfaction along the lines, and I
am heavy in tough times but very
light headed when lifetimes seem to
fly by. I am a mind, I am the attention
of details that strive for the extra
mile, I am a mind's eye view of what
one person can do to see the limits
are like the skies, I am to keep an
open mind as the sad there lies, the
good there shines through the
survival of the distance, of the weight,
of the time, I am a mind.

I am a touch

I am a touch, I am a sincere presence
that surrounds a gentle life, I am
found in someone's treasured chest
that is open ready to share a brush of
their light, and I am a sighing sound
that rest so sure from the touchy feely
of warm hands resting side by side so
much. I am a touch, I am given as a
confidence boost with an extra push, I
am received as a gift from the senses to
never give up in no way, no luck, no
such, and I am conceived from a wiser
that once said a magic touch can cure
that everyday bad stuff. I am a touch, I
am a drop of water so pure on the
forehead, I am a cross, a sign, a belief
to feel a higher love for, to be real sure
of, to be secure in life until fulfilled in
death so touched, I am a touch.

I am beautiful

I am beautiful, I am on the surface
and I am skin deep, I am a smile,
a purpose, a destiny, and I am shining
bright on purpose through life's
realities and rules. I am beautiful, I am
a wild flower, I am the rolling plains, I
am a light of endearment rising tall,
and I am a right of empowerment
surprising all. I am beautiful, I am a
wrinkle, I am a white hair, I am a
dimple, I am here, I am there, and I
am everywhere no matter how big or
small. I am beautiful, I am the old, I
am the new, I am the bold, I am to do
what I can to fulfill my talent, my call,
my all, I am beautiful.

I am blue

I am blue, I am the many shades
and hues, I am in a daze and
confused, and I am so true in some
ways yet in other ways I have a
feeling I am being used. I am blue,
I am the clear wide open skies so
huge, I am beneath the tides just
a whole other World for nature to
seek refuge, and I am in a nest, not
a robin, but a jay resting to lay the
eggs for life to be new. I am blue,
I am the sickness of the soul, I am
the music that releases the hold, yes,
I am the uplifting sadness from the
sounds of each note that is in check
and in tune. I am blue, I am the eyes
of some and behind the eyes of all, I
am the clouds in front of the sun as
the rain falls, I am a circle of light
surrounding the midnight moon, I
am to watch what I say, while others
get away with murder or I may be
sued, I am blue.

I am faith

I am faith, I am fond of a smile,
yes, I can be found for miles. I
am faith, I love, create, and fulfill
to redeem my place and God's Will.
I am faith, I spare no cost to live
through the best of my abilities I
give. I am faith, honestly trusted and
beloved, also charitable and very
thankful to the Lord above. I am
faith, I don't forget the good deeds
for the road less traveled always
leads. I am faith, if it were not for
happiness beyond the heartaches, for
gratefulness after the headaches, for
hugs through the pain, then the World
would be totally insane, but I am
Heaven sent, born from a higher form,
this is what I inspire to create, I
am faith.

I am inside

I am inside, I am underneath the
skin, I am the sea of blood rushing
through the veins, and I am the beat
box of love throbbing sweet songs
within. I am inside, I am the living
cells that made it all begin, I am
living well in a heavenly place from
a swell breath of fresh air, and I am
far away from the hellish ways with
a tell all tale of that great escape. I
am inside, I am a canvas of dark
reds and midnight blues inside I
am, I am an amazing priceless work
of art inside I am, and I am truly
the best creation of God's design,
the greatest masterpiece inside I
am, I am inside.

I am mercy

I am mercy, I am what God has on my soul, I am the thoughts for the sick, the hurt, and the bitter cold, I am the prayers for those dieing young and old, friends, and family. I am mercy, I am with the prisoners of war, I am about the worried civilians and their poverty stricken scars, and I am the shouts and screams for freedom in those restricted destinies. I am mercy, I am in the Middle East, I am in the North American countries, I am not a beast like you may have heard when they say mercy killings those words, instead I am the ease for the pain of the whole entire World truly. I am mercy, I am served day to day so Worldly, I am well deserved in every way so Earthly, I am a blessing for women, men, boys, and girls so Heavenly, I am mercy.

I am peace

I am peace, I am the calm approach
before and after a storm, I am the
silence then the cry when a newborn
baby is born, and I am in some form
inside of you and outside in many
ways too. I am peace, I am a sign, I
am a gesture, I am kind, I am a
messenger, and I am in a condition
to see eye to eye. I am peace, I am at
ease in a boat among the sea's
breeze, and I am a vote for beliefs
and dreams. I am peace, I am needed
to breathe a breath that is pure and
free. I am peace, I am as sure as I can
be, I am to explore beyond the eyes
of disbelief, I am deep therefore I
always give more, I am peace.

I am relentless

I am relentless, I am not giving up
on life or love, I am living it up and
reaching up for the pursuit of
happiness from above, and I am
going on each tiring way with
nothing more and nothing less, but
the best. I am relentless, I am doing
what needs to be done, I am the few,
the proud, the one able to withstand
the stress that seems to pile up more
and more instead of less and less. I
am relentless, I am nonstop through
the negative, I am on top of the
positive, and I am a drop of blood
given for the gift of life to be
endless. I am relentless, I am intense
with thoughts, I am immense within
the heart, I am what I can be through
the sands of time so effortlessly, I
am relentless.

Inside that counts

My savings account is extinct, not found.
My checking account is gone, not around.
The account of my love life can be a downfall
as other things surround, but after all the accounts,
it all amounts to what's inside that counts. Now,
it's time to turn some things around, if I work
really hard in return I found;
my new accounts are in tact, exact,
my credit accounts are on the map, a fact,
the account of my love life may be still and
at a stall as other things surround, but after all
the accounts, it all amounts to what's inside
that counts.

Inspiration

*Inspiration is true beauty, creates a face
of hope, makes one stronger, and helps
others along the weary roads. Inspiration
across the many ways, long days, and the
mixed feelings so hard to say. Inspiration
to bear one's cross, on the arm and in the
hand, to send the message of God's presence
is there so have no fear. Inspiration is the
answer to the plenty of questions asked.
Inspiration is the pretty face with the smile
that should never be masked. Inspiration
through every situation good or bad.
Inspiration to blink, to drink, to think of
what you have, or what can be had with
inspiration.*

It pours

When it rains about, then it pours all out.
They say I don't talk, I don't say much
at all, but isn't that what my life is for.
I think it said a lot so far. Life's too short
for all sorts of tall tale stories. So day to
day I'll keep it short and sweet. I'll just say,
"hey, what's up?" before I'll see you later
with no worries. That's me and I am more
than what you see. I consider myself a simple
person with a purpose to touch you from your
head to your feet poetically. That's the more
for sure you will see. "A picture is worth a
thousand words", they say. I say, "words
can express a thousand more in different ways."
Here I go, there I go, every where I will show,
my heartfelt emotions blazing with a stylish
artistic flow. So grab a hold of your chair, now
off we go. When it rains about, then it
pours all out.

Just be you

Make a smile, make a rainbow, make
anything worthwhile no matter which
way you go. Just do it now; later is not
in the picture. So trust that you know
how. Don't be someone else, just be
you and do what you want to do.
Make a point and shoot straight, make
a heartbeat faster, make something
worth the wait no matter how long it
takes. Only time can make it greater.
Don't be someone else; just be you.
Don't fright when it comes to you.
There will be a right turn or a left
turn, only you can tell what you
yearn for. Just remember don't be
someone else; just be you and do
what you want to do.

Measures

Another one's past is another one's
treasure, dust to dust plus ashes to
ashes, we pleasure one's trust
through rash and tough measures.
Another one's past is another one's
adventure, muster we must plus
justice we just, we assure one's
love through lust and rough measures.
The weather we weathered, yes all of
us together through favors we
favored, just so we can better the
bitter, and construct instead of
destruct through the awestruck
measures.

My gusto

When I'm feeling so-so and can't
find no more get up and go, then
I reach deep inside for my gusto.
In here it's like the Mirage Casino
in the sleepless city of Reno.
My heart is full of pyrotechnics to
keep me from what is hectic, so I
don't let go.
My mind is pulled apart to show
the lunatics all my adrenaline
mixed with info.
My body is an inferno ready to
glow so bright like a fanatic riding
the quick highs; yes, yes, and the
sick lows; no, no.
When I'm feeling so-so and can't
find no more get up and go, then
I reach deep inside for my gusto.

My heart's desire

My heart's desire is to start the fire within me.
So my heart burns with love, in return,
overheated feelings throughout my veins shoot
flames like a speeding train. As the heat melts
away my aches and my pain, those heat waves
reveal my heart's serenity, it's fiery destiny. So
amazingly, it's shining a tower of power. As it
rises higher and higher! Also brighter and brighter!
What a fire! Eternally set free, forever more, and
for all to see within me, the passion, the spirit, and
the true greatness that is now engulfing my
heart's desire.

Naturally

Please give no more, but take no
less, and always live for your best.
Just leave your stress with your mess
and forgive so you can rest well in
health, yes within yourself. If you
never felt your heart truly swell with
happiness, I hope your days will soon
be blessed naturally.
Please give no more, but take no
less, and always live for your best.
Just leave your stress with your mess
and forgive so you can rest well in
health, yes within yourself. If you
were never dealt your heart of
hearts from King to Queen, I wish
your relationship plan will soon
be blessed naturally.

Playing catch up

Falling behind, beginning with another
nickel and dime scheme. Always walking
around with your head down. When you look
up, it seems like you're always playing
catch up.
Some questions left at times unanswered,
later on, fit into our lives, it's unforgettable.
Just rise up to the test. Do your very best,
playing catch up.
Looking beneath, recovering from another
nickel and dime dream. Always running
around, searching for answers that can't
be found. When you think you found
them, it seems like you're always let
down. Fed up, playing catch up.
Sometimes answers left all alone,
later on down the road find their home.
Just rise up to the test. Do what you can.
As long as it's your very best,
playing catch up.

Scars

By far, it's so hard to let down the guard and open up those arms. So far, it's the scars that show us and open us up to who we are; giving or caring, loving or sharing, above all just daring us to stand up for what we are. So far, it's the scars that touch us and mean so much, they help us see who we are; living for something, giving for nothing, caring for anything, above all showing love for everything, that's what we are! By far, it's so hard to let down the guard and open up those arms. So far, the scars make up what we are. By far, the scars take us to who we are, our scars!

Single red rose

For a single red rose, it holds the
beautiful words untold, it shows
the pedals of love that unfold, and
it grows unity in both the roots of
trust and the stems of hope.
For such a commitment to be shown
in a single red rose, it's confidence
must be bold, and it's patience must be
sowed for it's existence to be known.
For a single red rose, it holds the
beautiful words untold, it shows
the pedals of love that unfold, and
it grows unity in both the roots of
trust and the stems of hope.

That path called hope

There are days I stare in a daze at the
chandelier lights. Unaware I'm drifting
some where along the sands of time. A grain
of pain felt is as real as a grain of sand being
melted into glass. Behold that great creation
is also held to make light shown. The destination
is truly endless and unknown. We are created
in the same way, I hope you know. We all have
capabilities, and the ability to show the meaning
of our being is on that path called hope. Yes, we
are created the same way, I hope you know. We are
all made with hopes and dreams, so it seems. It's
up to us to trust and to believe on that path
called hope. Our destination is truly endless and
unknown. The hesitations should be gone, so let
them go. No one is really all alone because
something or someone is drifting along that path
called hope.

The endless tanks

I have the thanks of a strong
mind and of a big heart,
however, along the times they
have fallen apart. If it wouldn't
be for the lengths within, I never,
before the strengths would have
taken it all in.
When, would it have been enough?
Like whenever, whatever, never mind,
it's so rough to think even with a
big hearty beat this life is still
so tough.
When, could it have begun then?
Whoever, said those broken
thoughts and changes of heart
should have sunk in while the
endless tanks of a strong mind
and of a big heart give thanks
again and again.

The fight

The struggles through the small battles
are assuring confidence. They all show
the scars, bruises, or bumps that life can
give. The confidence arises with each
forgiving heart that pounds a beat toward
the shining light found within the fight. The
conflicts through the big battles are reassuring
an alliance. They trigger your mind to use your
train of thought to defeat the evil, the pain,
and the hurt that surrounds the heroism,
therefore, redeeming the shining light that
once was lost, but is now found within
the fight.

The Hero

You are impressed that I am so strong
and that depression doesn't sing my
song. I see what you don't, here's my
trust beating the odds, the test, and the
stress, but the best sound from start to
finish and that's heard all around, it's
from my heart. I am blessed. Yes,
there's no ifs, ands, or buts about it
because I found a Hero within me. The
Hero that is within all of us, so just
trust, love, and lead. You can rest assure,
I know pain does hurt, but I show my
worth through my life's hard work, and
from what I write within my own words.
Plus I truly believe it's alright to see
less is more, but most of all I behold a
light, it's from my soul. I am blessed.
Yes, there's no ifs, ands, or buts about
it because I found a Hero within me. The
Hero that's within all of us, so just trust,
love, and lead.

The human race

I realize the human race is a fast pace, so I carry along hope and faith. When I am blind to see my destiny, I simply allow hope to guide me. When I am behind on my beliefs to be free, I thankfully give praise to faith for enlightenment on me. I compromise the human race with my give and take, so I hurry along togetherness and promise. When I am farseeing my future, I naturally follow togetherness to connect me. When I am hardly in my own nature, I gracefully allow promise to protect me. I realize I compromise the human race.

The measure of a Man

The measure of a Man, it's neither if he has
big or small hands, nor if he's of a tall or
small stance. No one seems to respect each
other, the Mother Nature of one another is
unique. The measure of a Man stands strong
when weak, takes pride in a job that he has
done, is always there with arms open wide for
his kids no matter what they did, and true
family and friends bring out this person
called Man. The measure of a Man is sure of
the lessons being taught. The moments that
can't be bought, but they are brought up in
memories. It's the history, the stories, the
fears, the glory, some what of a mystery,
until one looks past the material, the physical,
and one sees the individual, the spiritual,
that is the measure of a Man.

The miracle of growth

I don't have planter hands or a green thumb,
but here is my chance. I plant with my hands
pure love and more hugs than one can show
in my first rows. Also hope along another row
next to faith to help bless it from the pesky
bugs that can devastate. As I wait, I'm sure
the cure is not from miracle grow, no it's the
miracle of growth. On the other rows are
shown tenderness, greatness, and all the best,
yes to rise from the weathered test and stress.
All of these rows put together breathe, feed,
and lead the rest to what is better. There is
not a planter hand nor a green thumb that
can understand. As I wait, I'm sure the cure
is not from miracle grow, no it's the miracle
of growth.

The truth

The truth is ugly because it hurts you and me.
We could be so lucky to see the truth really
sets us free. Happy or not, our conscious can
breathe mentally. Then spiritually, the trust is
back on track within us. When we create lies,
the virus attacks us physically. Our bodies are
stressed, it's a must to rest, but passing the
test feels the best. That's when the truth is
ugly because it hurts you an me. It's up to us
to cross the deep red sea of envy, jealousy,
and greed. So don't dread being tossed across
each. It's then we can finally see that mentally,
spiritually, and physically, the truth can set
us free.

Threshold

So far away is the soul in a place that is so cold. The pain is unbearable as it grabs a hold, and wont let go. Faster the blood flows, harder the pulse grows, closer to becoming out of control. Beyond those signs another sign shows, welcome, the pain is now surpassing the threshold. So day after day the hurt does stay. So many pills for a worth, but it doesn't feel like any of them really work. The mind is confused, insane, and buzzerk, the thoughts are used like an old worn out shirt, the rest of the body feels abused within the field of hurt. Beyond those times the next time shows, welcome, the pain is now surpassing the threshold.

Truth Serum

*Is there any answer to my life's cancer? I know there is fun,
but down it goes the truth serum. As it shows the highs and
the lows along these well known roads, I still loose focus and
I get real cold when reality is not so great. When I am served
more insanity from the vanity plate. I am suppose to
understand the circumstances, but at times I can't seem to
truly comprehend them. It's not right, all the doses of pain I am
living in. The poisoning of my life just to see the bright light, I am
getting pale, a taste that is stale, as the World serves me another
undeserving poisoned cocktail. I know there is fun, but down
goes the truth serum. This makes me surreal and takes me sailing
away from my family and my friends. It's hard to feel, as my arms
are open just like my hands, and I spin in circles again and again. I
am left wondering, is there really a new beginning or is here truly
the end? Is there any answer to my life's cancer? Where's the coke
and rum and all that fun in this truth serum?*

Unexpected inspiration

Inspiration is an immense feeling of beauty,
boldness, and hope. I get these feelings when
I am touched and blessed with a vision that's
unexpected. It gives me a way to create a
picture of poetry. A flower for example is
always seen in a garden or in the wild fields.
However, there is one way that I would go
where I noticed the struggle of nature in the
crack of a walkway. The Earth and the sun
must have sowed an immense feeling to a
seed, and the roots must have became blessed
to feed because in time a stem sprouted up. I
passed by every chance to get a glance at the
seed being touched by every step of nature. In
the end the pedals unfolded to behold a flower
in the crack of the walkway. It struggled to
create beauty, boldness, and hope that's
unexpected inspiration.

Ways, shapes, and forms

I heard words in a vague scream like a cry,
saying aloud, "but we try, we try." Those
words seem to echo a sound that is so
profound to me, as I see everybody really is
down, so down. We need a rescue party to
find us and remind us that this craziness will
go away. So here I am today, ready to say,
"Friends, when you can't bend no more then
I will lend you my hand because we have all
been here before in many different ways,
shapes, and forms." Whether it be broken
homes, broken hearts, broken dreams with
nowhere to start. We need a search party to
guide us and enlighten us from the craziness
within every day. So here I am today, ready
to say, "Friends, when you can't stand no
more then I will send you my strength because
we have all been there before in many different
ways, shapes, and forms."

Welcome home

I learned to be focused on the importance of family. A secured home shows where values, respect, and laughter is strong. I always say the best is made the home grown way. Yes, the door is secure and for sure the light always stays on in the living room. So when family is sick, hungry, tired, and/or thirsty then welcome home. When family has joy, passion, smiles, and cheer, listen here, welcome home. The temple where we grew up, the seat where we can always go, it's all traced back to that place called home. Even the mat I stand on, in front of the opened door, still focused on the importance of family, it says, welcome home.

Willpower

What does it take? When everything is at
stake, whether sweet or sour on every
minute there hides another hour.
Willpower is the drink,
willpower is what I think,
willpower to show you and you, my heart,
willpower is the beat that goes off the charts.
What does it take? When everything is on
the brake, whether speechless or really louder
on every step there rises another tower.
Willpower is in my tank,
willpower is what I drank,
willpower to flow through and through, my heart,
willpower to behold my finish when I start.
Willpower!

You are not alone

When the loss is great, when the feelings
are costly, and when there is mostly wrong
to the point of why me. You are not alone
because faith is overflowing. There's trust
along the river beds, there's hope among
the warm streams, and there's love within
the deep ocean seas. So believe me, I'm
sure, you are not alone, just like water is
pure. When the hurt breathes, then the
trust bleeds, and all the hope and the love
flows purity, inside and outside, to show
the ways are strong and life goes on, we
belong, you are not alone.

Illuminations

360 Degrees

An emotion filled with life will strive
as long as there are oceans of hope with love inside.
A commotion will chill with a feel to divide
so remember free will at those times that multiply.
There still will be a spill or a feel that's taken away
but we can always add a touch to make the day.
Whether a brush, a hug, a word of love and trust
those are all together or one by one a plus.
Along the twist and the turns under the weather
the weak shall go on stronger and the meek shall get better.
For if it wouldn't be for the Earth, moon, and the seas
then our emotions would be at a standstill instead of 360
degrees.

A Call

The lights are dim and the dark circles are around,

the way seems so far away to be found.

The right feelings surround but can't choose a direction,

the reasons bruise, confuse, and lose a connection.

If you have been through any of this,

it can get better only if you wish.

Death is something we all have to face

when we realize we are all a part of the human race.

Life is a thing of beauty to believe and behold,

so let us cherish every moment that is new and old.

Together we can turn a light among the dark of it all,

forever we can feel a reason, a connection, a direction, a call.

A Father and My Sun

I know what marriage and divorce with kids are all about
as I followed the highs and lows all of it beyond a doubt.
Those choices held within did come out
to express peace, some thought I was without.
My life decisions were a tough test to digest
no matter how hard and rough I allowed my best.
My price at times so priceless, I know I paid for it.
My fights would show a go, no guess to ever quit.
My mind does rest, my heart doesn't stress,
my soul is set free to see more even when there's less.
So, the world turns to the unforgiving trend with lost kids again,
as my world burns a father and my sun on my daughters till no end.

A New Start to Begin

A found but lost feeling, felt within,
when there is an end even with a new start to begin.
The search is for a spark from anything
then the flash of light can show something.
The thought would mean a vision to reflect
and to realize all the decisions do connect.
Why not look inside for an emotion to detect
the idea is alive and living with respect.
My wandering sent forth what came next
within each simple breath became life so complex.
A found but lost feeling, healing within,
when there is an end even with a new start to begin.

A New Thought

The words still traveling
through my heart unraveling
the parts of tragedies
to show a love of happenings.
Apparently, the words run deep
attached by the feelings of peace
while the emotions hold so strong
the mind, the body, the soul do belong.
What was thought of as an end,
that unraveling of traveling God sent
were the words of faith to begin
a new life, a new thought, amen!

A Part

The darkest days wonder around
they lurk from a distance then come down.
The minutes and hours cannot be placed
this is where a life becomes misplaced.
Along that way the stress comes to play
here and there one lingers in the dark of every day.
The path had created a hold
until one falls apart to become whole.
The bright colors start to come together from tears
the salty waters wash away the dark fears.
The stand has brought new days full of heart
to make time, love, and life so much a part.

A Scenery of True Beauty

I believe together you and me
we can see a scenery of true beauty.
After all the biggest difference in a major tragedy
comes from holding hands for peace and unity.
If one teaches about hope and something of love
there may be nothing below but far reaches those above.
Things do go south with a tick and tock it is heard of
so look up to the sky winter time is for the doves.
Things do warm up to a degree that is great
so shook up that is why summer time is in good faith.
Among you, me, and the weather makes three
within our lives' routines is a scenery of true beauty.

A Work of Art

I learned a marriage does not survive by ones
hard work alone. I thought a marriage unites as
it grows to behold a work of art. So I fought to sow,
feed, and tend those rows. The needs were met, but her
forecast had regrets. At last there was too much water
and too much sun. It happened too fast to lose such
wonder and to lose such fun. My experiences, my
emotions, hence forth my notions, that this once a
marriage is buried within the ocean. Not for things I
hadn't tried to bear nor for reasons I hadn't tried to
care. Otherwise, the land that once began to thrive,
ended up, swallowed up by her cheating tides.
Allowing what I planted and tended so hard with my
hands, to be nothing more but salty water and sand.
I would have never known the marriage would part,
however, those emotions buried within the ocean
behold a work of art.

All in the Name of

My stomach turns and my heartburn starts
so much to digest as I learn the fires of my heart.
I know some things will never change
and I know other things will never be the same.
I believe a light burns so deep internally
and can be set free to see externally.
So inflamed along the inspired rites of passage
only to stumble across a deeper message.
Those feelings real plain with power said to shine
in that yellow and to glow within that red light.
My wrath's fire below, sent higher flames above,
love now will be seen brighter all in the name of.

Cain and I am Abel

I like to do what I feel is right
but along the way there's always another sight.
What I see is dark and there's wrong
following me, tagging along, singing its song.
So I allow myself the gray to be at one
because after the dark I remember there's a sun.
Once the feeling has passed, at last the light,
and I am aware the gray was neutral among the fight.
It's here I see again what has been earned,
it's here I believe in the lessons being learned.
While I feel it was right within the open field so capable
I believe what I faced was Cain and I am Abel.

Collette

It's a gloomy day as I see within irises,
many spirits I admire that hold true desires.
Afflicted with cancer to the tune of a debt,
so we walk for a cure to save lives from death.
Many march to a beat to beat the needles and wires,
with the love and the hope that inspires the entire.
Still this one in particular I shall never forget,
as she held a big light so polite, her name Collette.
Her mother and I work together so I hear of the fight.
I pray for them all especially her and her life.
The cancer has taken a strong hold and just won't let,
Now the sun rises like everlasting light from irises of Collette.

Dear God

Back on the high seas is my will
to ask what is real constantly until.
As the next wave I ride glides
toward the highest peak in the sky.
Once there I will ask God why
the kind of why that eyes can't lie.
The world is at a loss for words
why dear God aren't we as high as the birds?
Why do we hide when we should seek,
and can you open our eyes to belief?
Back down to see seas rush like his blood in us
a heartbeat echoes my trust is the real moral compass.

Father's Rights

If you find your love life doesn't turn out right
but you have kids, don't give up on that fight.
A relationship with their mother may have been fool's gold
however, remember their little minds, hearts, and souls.
Fathers you can have more of a connection
defend, honor, and respect your custody visitation.
From my experiences I seen my little girls in the rough
become polished up, so bright among my days and my nights, it's love.
Life is so short for me to be without mine
after all those diamonds of my eyes are one of a kind.
If I unroll my map, could you be truly driven
to close the gap for father's rights are a fact not opinions.

Find Meaning in this World

Instead of spending money on value
shouldn't we spend time with love on values?
If we lie, steal, and cheat, isn't that immoral,
so why don't we see, believe, and fulfill our morals?
Why do we look for something so demeaning,
when some have nothing yet still shines true meaning.
Why do we cast aside a good idea, why reject it,
when we deny change only to complain and don't accept it.
If we are given everything on Earth for no hard work
then why should we believe in anything or its worth.
Instead of acting on something that's so absurd
shouldn't we come together to find meaning in this world?

Fish

I like to fish, but I am not the fisherman
even though you fish does not make you the fisher of man.
I give up all that I can again even to fish
but Lord I don't break out ahead in the end, I wish.
I do it all over again friend
and time after time try to understand.
It's when the rod does rest in the wind
You see the reel still does tend to spin.
These true roots are within seas depth which
the tides that bind are the real itch.
Together as a sea of people among the land
forever we fish deep for those freedoms within.

Flashback

I overheard in a distant conversation
the world use to be a blank canvas for an imagination.
I believe the poor always dream bigger
but do the rich dream poor or lower figures.
I hope what triggers the dream isn't greed
as if the grand scheme of things create the creed.
So, the love about the heart on the line
cast its ripple effect from dream to life.
Every action donates to the great contribution
still money takes away from a soul's institution.
I said after what I heard don't back track
moving on we all can live the dream then flashback.

For All

The pain will always be here
after the loss of love one feared.
The hurt place still etched in memory
will be blessed in the name of Mary.
The loss has taken a piece away
but the void makes room to fulfill each day.
The time shines a change of face
that clock hands gently touch with faith.
The belief will test our hands
because the grief still feels like the end.
The pain is shared from all
within love, of life, in death for all.

Forgiveness and The Truth

I am dumbfounded as I find forgiveness within hands of time
and I believe it was always around ticking by.
The kindness may have been hiding behind deception
but eye for an eye I do realize it's all about perception.
One's right is one's wrong as along those differences
I see the truth does long its existence.
I vowed that I wouldn't change a tear or a trouble
and somehow the fear became a friend with no struggle.
Every step did connect toward the biggest goal
which was to share with the disconnected my heart and my soul.
In the beginning I know not what to do from me to you
but I followed time to find forgiveness and the truth.

Frostbite

A transformation from water to snow
is a translation for uncle not to go.
His desire to visit family that night,
would be a path to see his light.
His kindness, compassion, and love, old friend I describe.
I will never forget every morning Uncle Paul,
especially the morning with family after his call.
His destination rest in the hands of God above,
as a boy getting attention from this man I'll miss his love.
My first time to lose someone so close, it's not right,
but from my memory I remember his light and that time of
frostbite.

I come to Believe

Love can be bigger than me,
hope can be deeper than any sea.
Trust can extend beyond hand to hand
belief can with stand the grains of sand.
Drive can make the impossible so possible
faith can create a time, water, and apostles.
Destiny can happen for a reason,
change can awaken any season.
Light can redeem all in one,
life can shine bright as the sun.
Together within all of these to be
we must become I come to believe.

I Feel the Need to be Strong

I wish I was weak in my beliefs,
I wish I would find a need to please.
I don't beg, borrow, or steal,
I don't act like the type that is not real.
Then again maybe I should do all of this
after all these many have found bliss.
I wish I was more than,
I wish I couldn't defend the enemy just friends.
I do hurt, blurt, and feel deserted,
I do over react to words said to hurt me.
Then again maybe I should go along the wrong,
but instead I feel the need to be strong.

In the Heart of a Town

I am standing here looking down
glancing up then staring around.
I am not one for falling in a depression
unlike the city that has fallen in recession.
My breath however deep in motion
knows that deeper feeling and emotion.
A simple thought to hold onto finds a home
as the heart adds a sound so it's not alone.
On the outside so much pride to buy
but out of sight is how to unite.
It's no wonder why I am looking down,
after all, my world is in the heart of a town.

Into the Painted

I see a painted image depicted to show
a cross on a stain glass window.
At times I'm lost and don't know
in my confusion which way to go.
The bumps along the narrow road
make it unclear on what to behold.
I slowly stand as if it hurts so
to take a step forward to break a hold.
I end up in the center of a crossroad
in the same spot feels like a moment ago.
I see an image it's the picture of Satan
I move across not lost into the painted.

Life Within Emotions

I am hit with waves of strong emotion
that didn't sit well like sickness in motion.
A kid wondering why hi's and goodbye's took place
from deadly disease to the miracle of a new face.
A teenager of accolades catches a breath
for an elder with emphysema couldn't get.
An adult filled with choices of regret
as another fulfilled those choices till death.
A family together has broken apart, because of insane pains
while some are forever a part of love within the same veins.
On this trip among the sea like strong motions
we are all aboard to see life within emotions.

Like an Inmate

The sunrise has not risen
still I'm awake feels like prison.
The shackles I unhappily carry
with those chains I'm not so savvy.
My time is trying to get by
in this life sentence ending with why.
The hard ways in the workplace so far
showed the court those low bars on how far.
Would I see the up side scheme
so I could believe the outside dream?
The day's emotions struggle with little cents
feeling like an inmate behind four walls makes no sense.

March

I hear the sounds of a march
the wonderful pounds in the month of March.
It is so heart beating and pulsating
on this morning of love for racing.
The men and women on downtown streets
with children running around tirelessly.
They come to take part in a big way
to share their thoughts on this a big day.
If I learned one thing from all of this
we are one piece of the puzzle that fits.
The reason is so heartwarming and pure
to come together to march for a cure.

Me and Health

Sit and wait for a purpose yet faint
to feel this way as I await
for another pill so tasty
slow motioning such as a turtle racing.
All that my health transpires
are severe medical issues and wires,
popped veins, mood swings, pain not for hires
beckon there ways burning bright fires.
I pause those many seconds believing
because believing in nothing is not leaving
me and health are in the midst of conceiving
all this time we sit with real pain believe me.

Mr. Thirsty

Another step forward feels so backed
in a moment I will be pushed to step back.
It is so difficult these times, positively what
when the man with no heart there positively sucks.
I am not a part of the dead beat fad
so Uncle Sam pulls at the heart of this single dad.
The wheels spin in the world of heartache like it does
as my little girls understand more than grown-ups.
It's hard to be angry when everything seems mad
it takes too much energy when you're hungry and feel had.
Why should I accept the negative change with sincerity
when positive change can feed this poverty and quench Mr. Thirsty?

My Candle Burning

Do you believe in what's wild,
do you feel the love in a smile?
In a hope and in a prayer I do,
in a ghost and in a light do you?
Do you breathe in the dark,
do you see where there's a spark?
In a dreaming destiny I do,
in a steam and in a street do you?
Do you need what is real,
do you mean what you feel?
In a moment and in a yearning I do,
I hold true my candle burning for you.

My Place

I could paint a picture called a work of art
or I could write a poem that touches a heart.
I can show my offspring all of my love
because that is something I am just as sure of.
I see my abilities that make my world
and I believe in my capabilities and my little girls.
I did not know that I could do what I have shown
but I learned the hard ways and have grown.
I may not be college bound or from the streets,
however, this country boy works and plays as hard for keeps.
After all I am grateful and appreciate the unknown
because where I have been, my place is well known.

My Real World

The world is feeling the cost
finally I don't feel so lost.
I never wished this on anyone
at least I don't seem like the only one.
Those close and far feel every pinch yes
for a single father with two kids have been into many inches.
Sacrifice is to control the means
this is what I live by any means.
If I don't have it is alright
it's not what I lack but what I like.
I like to overcome the struggles of pressure
so world welcome to my real world rest assured.

My Senses

My eyes see more within wrong then right
that is when I belong and life is out of sight.
My ears listen real hard to every painful sound
even though my heart beats so very loud.
My fingers feel the burning sensations that can touch
within my compassion and attraction of poetry and such.
My taste buds open up to the dark spices of life
as I pour a cup of love for a recipe that's light.
My nose can smell the fear a mile away
so I follow until I'm near to make my way.
My time spreads faith throughout all my senses hence
creating my destiny about the senseless quenches.

My Sky

I carry my burdens real high
upon my shoulders that's why,
I need to release that hurt goodbye
among the breeze from I.
I fill the clouds with my cries
in return they sympathize,
I know now by this time why
the atmosphere here is compromised.
I feel the peace back inside
when my weight is free outside,
when at the height is a rainbow slide
it's then I thank a good friend, my sky.

Natural World

There behind the oak trees
passing though the spring breeze
a resting picture on the grass
because the clouds are not overcast.
The hollow figure following you
that mimics your every move
has a tender touch on cement,
but burning your bare feet makes you swear a comment.
The shapes and sizes of the days
they made their way from place to place.
All of these images do show
the natural world that lives by shadows.

Never Skipped a Real Beat

When you're feeling blue
from aches and pain too.
Here is what to do
to make it right on through.
Close your eyes real tight
believe your will and your might.
Even when you're too ill
hope, love, and trust just will.
When you're in a daze from pills
beyond the purple haze are thrills.
Up and down your spine feels the heat
as your fight never skipped a real beat.

Path to Forgiveness

Living within the outs and without an inn is

a woman traveling about the path to forgiveness.

A virgin carrying the son of the Lord, and

searching for shelter among the man's land.

Wandering to a barn where no one is at,

delivering the joy of the world where sheep sat.

The word of this birth spreads to connect,

like a caring word in a verse said to protect.

As this boy grew into a man named Jesus,

He builds with his hands a religion to save us,

even a skeptic can turn a corner to feel,

the hard times yearn for hope and God to heal.

Plant

There are hands that can plant
those dreams from the sky and of our land.
They take an inspiration of hope
the way the seed takes a hold.
They make a difference to some
like the rain and light form the rays of the sun.
They create food for thought
in the same way the roots and the stems brought.
They show a passion so courageously fought
like the plant home grown and not store bought.
There are those hands that can
share those dreams they plant.

Quality or quantity

Some people just want more things that is no lie.
Some people need some things and they are
satisfied. It's how we live our lives, win or
lose; pick and choose, either quality or quantity,
but don't confuse the two. We must learn from
the burdens, so few do. We need to see the
bridges burn, then rebuild trust over the
feelings of blue. It's how we see it through,
win or lose; pick and choose, whether quality or
quantity, but don't confuse the two.

See Life in a T-shirt

When you feel your eyes burn
even in a squint it's a blind hurt.
You have so much with free will
every breath is every bit free until.
You want to walk away to leave
every step you take you can't see.
So you decide to stay to breathe
so you can find a way to believe.
Your sight is away from the naked eye
you look for insight within visible light.
You realize all this time it was dirt
a sleeve to wipe your eyes to see life in a t-shirt.

Self-Served

Welcome to the high priced fuel station
where you do deposit your check throughout the nation.
I can't believe how much, so much cost
at the pumps it doesn't pay to be lost.
I believe the government has some wrong-doing but as
I was saying they lost their way with gas.
The fumes burn our distant eyes, then surprise
another ten cents to cause us not to jet ride.
What is the deal, is it to steal us blind
because I feel these times have crossed that line?
We are so far from where we need to be well served
let it start with lowering gas prices, it is still self-served.

Shepherd's Voice

I can be lost along the lands with no plans or
I can pay a cost then open my hands again,
that is my choice. I can die trying to figure out
what this life is for or I can compromise and
be wise to what life has in store that is my choice.
But, when I heard a Shepherd's voice from a
distance tending sheep, in an instant I found no
resistance. He spoke to me of a seed and then
told me to lead others to a bright light with a
field of dreams. Now, I finally see that I can
grow and be anything I want to be. Wow, there
is a middle ground between the ups and the
downs. That is where I found my voice, that is
where I planted my seed, indeed, that brought
me to me. Thanks to the choices I made by
listening to the Shepherd's voice.

So Deep Under

Through the earth's shattering thunder
and the words of chattering wonder,
I still carry my peace within me
along with my love to be so free.
Beyond the painstaking storms
and those insane taking up arms,
I will happily make my stand
among my heart I hold in hand.
For if it wouldn't be for the plunders
and if it wouldn't be for the blunders,
then what I feel would be no wonder
among the words that touch so deep under.

Speak with Poise

I can be so confused when lines cross
because I was taken wrong now all seems lost,
I see when there is nothing wrong at all
it seems I get asked, what's wrong, off the wall.
I notice when there is something not right
I don't hear is everything alright?
Life becomes in between those who care for nothing
and those who dare to create something out of nothing.
We have so many outlets for communication
but I guess it's easier to over use the imagination.
In a world that is so far away from a voice
I pray we fix the crossed lines, really care and speak with poise.

Tears of Joy

Waters of the sea as they release
waves of relief along my cheeks.
Emotions so big like the oceans they rise
to fill my eyes with those salty streams of surprise.
Those water paths that fall down my face,
they are emotions of joy that have found a place.
The fears have floated by
to allow my happy cry.
I realized before I was to prevail a man,
I was to sail through the grief the best I can.
Now that I am no longer a boy,
"Wow!" I can see through my tears of joy.

The Blueprint

When someone makes you feel special inside,
the belief and the reason doesn't need to hide.
No self pity will be a part of any concern
also nobody else can cool your burn.
Totally and whole hearted be yourself
so emotionally, physically, and mentally all is well.
The focus and direction should show tunnel vision
for the love and connection will go through a troubled decision.
While you hold the lines and the walls to worth,
life will mold the minds and the calls to work.
That someone who made you feel like an original true ink,
that real special feeling for you are the blueprint.

The Design

Everyone is unique within his or her own design
with genes, physique, and thoughts in mind.
Precious is the deliverance for all the different kind
within a drop of water since the beginning of time.
As cultures, color, and creed drew the line
the belief that we are all one still must shine.
The victory, the defeat, and the divine
shall cast its light, its shadow, and its lifetime.
The seconds, minutes, hour, days, and years that fly by
they happen so fast that it has to be a crime.
Even when you don't know, time feels slow, you find a bind
it's the history, the family, the glory of the design.

The Distance

There are soft steps that are placed
along the hard cement walk ways.
Somewhere the tough times still grind
out there among the good kind.
There are sweet notes of music
where sour doses feed the sick.
Somewhere the long lines still divide
over there the open doors fill up inside.
There are many living in the big cities
where others on the countryside pinch pennies.
Somewhere here or there life is as in existence
where the maze creates the distance.

The Main Subject

At times we all need a release from all of it
the stress, the mess, and the guess of what if.
So let the tears keep those fears outside
then listen, hear, and start to rebuild inside.
The process won't pass like the speed of sound,
instead the steps will come with leaps and bounds.
As the guilt, the hurt, and the bad peels the negative,
the hills, the work, and the sad reveal the positive.
The realization there's only one life to live
should make one prove what they have to give.
Once the worse is laid to rest, to forgive, but not to forget
going forward will shed some light on the main subject.

The Picture in Frame

If you take a picture in your mind,
is it to see the world with a different eye?
Do you view the signs along the weary streets?
Few take the time to follow their eerie beat.
It doesn't hurt to look for those who are needy
after all that is what gives us true meaning.
Really observe the elders, no medicine, needing shelter
or the teenagers with cell numbers, and paging Helter Skelter.
Truly serve the children much love and caring feelings,
reassure the unhappy people not capable of comprehending or dealing.
If you are one willing to make a greater change,
stop looking away so you can keep the picture in frame.

The Shots

I heard something so explosive
that triggered the negative and the positive.
The loud showers cleared to let us give
what the hours feared didn't forgive.
That day of thunder shook pocket books
while the lightning enlightened the crooks.
The raw emotions had no place to be cooled
before we saw a shadow we were fooled.
The draw was at a wind or at a fire
the positive drew a breeze so much lighter.
The negative so confused on the run
drew the shots that burned like the sun.

The Swords

We can defeat ourselves by defeating others,
or we can create a better place for one another.
The difference is all so relevant
when peace can send what hate can't.
The hurt is a domino effect of regret
because it is hard to see and to forget.
Amends can mend a broken land
when the heart is still beating with no end.
The words should pierce the soul to show
the fierce yet powerful feelings we hold.
If one can believe inside the meaning through worlds
the constitution is belief the pen is mightier than the swords.

To Get By

I count on hope within the sands of time,
I rely mostly on faith to satisfy my mind.
I believe in the best for all of mankind,
I breathe like all the rest just to get by.
I spread my seed to flower a life,
I shed my beliefs to power a light.
I pray real hard to end sickness, poverty, and wars,
I say how I feel with my wittiness, poetry, and scars.
I reflect on each day as it were my last,
I expect the unexpected among the present, future, and past.
I bleed my ink when I think of an emotion,
I need to bring it to life in a blink of an eye's motion.

What I sacrifice

I think twice at the price
I blink my eyes at life.
I wink at a pleasant sight
I use ink to express what I write.
As I believe the deepest light
comes from a place on the inside.
So I breathe to echo what is bright
till it shines a voice that is I.
It works when I think twice
for my worth is too priceless to be priced.
As my words blend within your sky
the world I believe in is what I sacrifice.

Where I Am At

I make a point to do what I can and can't
because I believe that is why I was sent.
I take a road to behold my place
so I can meet face to face with face.
I create a path to plant my seeds
then I wait and rest on Sabbath to see the deeds.
I am real simple with smiles within my environment
but I can somehow feel caught up in a moment.
I understand time can enable a safe haven
as I comprehend the safest time tables turn toward a Heaven,
I know beyond the questions and answers are the facts
that is why I retrace my steps to show where I am at.

Word

I heard a single word
that I will never forget
because the action
that took place was the best.
That word I could never tell
if it was a reaction
or did it echo within as well.
So it found a warm place
it simmered it dwelled
it grew only to find
it was only in the other's mind.
So that word from the start
eventually grew brittle and apart,
however, still believing in only one's heart
that word!

Words Brake

Some words have no meaning
when there's no action breathing
when there's more attraction misleading
those words lack their feeling.
There's no meaning behind words
when they're left all alone and unheard
when they're right in front of words unsaid
those words rest in one word deathbed.
Mean less words left behind
regardless if lost or couldn't find
the meaning for all time sake
is no meaning until words brake.

Perceptions

A Parent, apparently

I'm a parent with a childish grin. Apparently, I'm chasing after laughter by tickling and making silly faces for my kids. With my warm embraces, they release my love and my happiness so they are no longer hidden. This is my time where being goofy is living, a smile is forgiving, a touch is giving, a little while seems forever for my children. These places, those moments, that my reality can see. They are in many ways, those days my Mom and Dad showed me, how to be a parent, apparently.

A Speck

I am but a speck within the scheme
floating around in the current air stream.
Thanking God for living a dream
while surrounded by true friends and family.
A blot on the slide ready to show
the spot where veins release a flow.
The mark that's a permanent ink plan
not by one's hand but sent from the Lord's hand.
An itch into a state that isn't specific
a dot from the Atlantic to the Pacific.
Resting so small even magnified with specs
within the scheme I am but a speck.

All I want

I don't want to fit in with you
all I want is just to be and to do.
I don't want a misunderstood look
all I want is love and the Good book.
I don't want your pity for me
all I want is trust so let it be.
I don't want a deaf ear to hear me
all I want is a warm beating heart near me.
I don't want your grief or tricks
all I want is to be free as time ticks.
I don't want to see selfishness or be called a name
all I want is caring hands praying in the name.

Be told Life

I did not understand life
until I heard a rhyme.
I did not know the price
but then I learned why.
The words I sacrifice
await my heart, soul, and mind.
There is no surprise so wise
be hold beloved be told life.

Beyond any notion

I have been in worse conditions
to curse the plenty of hard decisions.
I have faulted in my words before
only to find solace at my heart's door.
I have pressed on through the dark pit
and passed the temptations of all of it.
I have hurt myself physically, mentally, spiritually and
I have yet to give in or see an end.
I have pondered the wrongs and the rights
as I plant my feet firm and set my sights.
I have been in a deep potion of commotion
to see myself wise beyond any notion.

Bridges

Burning bridges
instilling visions
bringing decisions
rebuilding bridges
learning conditions
living ambitions
crossing bridges
making impressions
taking directions
following bridges.

Day and Night

I behold a way for hope to stay
within the positive light I am the day.
The sunrise for my offspring to shine
with confidence and love to bloom their mind.
The rays that warm all those cold times
we are along those ways of our lives.
Until we strain our eyes, she is the night,
I am alone and my offspring fade out of sight.
Her nature took control of their self esteem
negativity lingers in the air they now breathe.
Darkness cast over the days as light fights night
the offspring struggle to see both day and night.

Drive

You and I push to rise
to leap toward new heights.
You and I work hard and try
to see forward new sights.
You and I can understand to compromise
to heed with a plan for it will be alright.
You and I again can arise
to fall my friend is to see a light.
You and I need to be wise
to use every ounce of our might.
You and I will breeze by
to live a driven life so drive.

Felt after a Drought

Today has such a big cloud
within my sky without a doubt
the heavy dark gray does surmount
in a way one way with no stop.
The day this day rain will drop
dew that drips along my mouth
the few I spill right on out
is the most felt after a drought.

Focus

The pain, the loss, and the cost of us
beyond, through, and above the dust,
it shows the path to help plus
goes to the depths to connect us.
We all want, need, and feel beloved
as we live, breathe, and heal with love,
it knows the wrath to overwhelm us
because it flows with ease untouched to touch.
The hand of the woman, the man, of trust
in time, in life, in love is less than much
so the fact is not the concept of lust
nor the definition of love it's us taking focus.

Forever Dad

My number, my turn
no numbness, my burn
none the less a return
within the seas out of this urn
ashes to ashes, dust to dust
forever Dad, the boat Captain returns.

Guest

I see a house well built on a hill
must have a strong foundation not of silt.
Then I see the walls bring the tension
only the false self bothers to pay attention.
When the struggles prove to be too much
the temper tends to bruise the touch.
The house well built produced no home
for the true self of family became a drone.
The noise of laughter was disapproved
because the sturdy walls silenced the good mood.
A house is a house just like you guessed
a home is where the heart is a welcomed guest.

Happily ever after for all

Once upon a rhyme before these times
words had so much power they caused crimes.
It isn't a joke when women couldn't vote
when African Americans riding a bus were provoked.
Remember when leaders had common sense
when a big bol gum and a tootsie roll cost a cent.
Back then entertainment was making a silly face
your friends were down the road you had no MySpace.
I remember when holidays brought family together
but now a day's every other holiday my kids and I are together.
A lot of things have changed like summer into fall
raising our heads up high praying happily ever after for all.

I never knew

I never knew death until I lived
I never knew pain could be a gift.
I saw a tear I never knew existed
when I felt my first born I was lifted.
I never knew happiness until I cried
I never knew loyalty but then I lied.
I heard wisdom laughing at my try
when my mistake took all with my pride.
I never knew peace until I saw wars
I never knew passion could leave scars.
I taste the good so sweet, the bad so bitter too
life's after taste so bitter sweet I never knew.

I thank God

I see people falling on their knees
from despair they are begging please.
It's so hard to be someone true
when the doors close on me and you.
We run around half the time lost
the other half standing still because of cost.
The Sunday of prayer is always here
yes, I say everyday prayer can adhere.
The workplace, school, governments create separation,
they don't mix religion day by day where's the deep connection?
I see the mess, feel the stress, I hear oh my God
as I kneel to pray day to day I thank God.

In a box

I hold a treasure of memories
which I carry everywhere close to me.
There's an old picture framed that my mind made
with our family so young, yea, out of date.
Here are the foot prints of my oldest girl
those painted imprints that created my world.
Another picture from my wedding day of course
I can't forget those moments among the harsh divorce.
The many downs that found ups hanging around
the friends riding with boom sounds in my town.
The little things and big stuff that's me on top
it all does echo nonstop found in a box.

In a snapshot

In a snapshot life can be a straight
shooter, a tear jerker, an ungrateful bruiser,
a top notch winner, or a hot scotch loser.
In a snapshot many images form, from each
picture the memories are born again.
In a snapshot the feelings of hard times churn,
the old places and younger faces return, the
family photos grow as the tables turn,
and to live is to learn in a snapshot.

In spite

In spite I can see but it's blurry
a double edge sword and it worries me.
On one side life is dull with sorry
on the other side life has much pride and glory.
This explanation from the sword I heard before
but my feelings made the connection bleeding more and more.
An incision cut real deep, the strain pours,
I feel a strange sense falling onto the floor.
I stumble to raise myself from my demise
to stare in the mirror a reflection within my eyes.
I see within a truth each edge has the might
I feel real deep my love caress the sword in spite.

In the dark night

Your memory erasing and gone for too long
so I keep memories home sweet home.
The space where the good times remain there
that place I swear I will always share.
Those times dealt with in life, love, and laughter
those ways I felt your light above disaster.
It was hard to see you confused with age
but in my heart we were on the same page.
If only memory could serve you and me right here again in that light
instead it hurts to see you lose the thoughts in the dark night.
The disease is but a lover's tragedy
to see a loved one forget whom they love to see.

Into Positive

When I am positive I feel moved
the negative disapproves, but I am in a groove.
The eyes can only see what is hectic
but I believe life can be so poetic.
The positive can redeem the view
to live the inner strength that's true.
The negative can take away the chase
to keep you down in a darker place.
The sights should reach deep inside
for the lights help each to see why.
The guilty conscious tells us all to give
to forgive, to live pass the negative into positive.

Is love

When push comes to shove
all I know to show is love.
My pain gets tossed aside
as my heart shelters, but does not hide.
I care without a thought in my mind
as I catch the love falling behind.
I give myself in those times
by helping, not pushing, but reaching lives.
I compromise emotions and feelings so much
with no regret for the gratitude at best is love.

Life Savings

Bad things break us and make us scared
with empty hearts and thoughts I swear.
What is left in our hands is up to us to understand.
Tough times they really tear me up again and again.
That is when enough is enough but then it still seems
to rip me apart till I cannot stand it.
They say a miracle will save us. I get that
saying but I been waiting and praying for my
day of life savings.
I try like you do to put the broken pieces
together, to weather the storms, to better myself,
and to open my arms. What I get in the end
at times I cannot comprehend. Rough times
they really shake me up enough but then it still seems
to take me apart till I cannot stand it.
They say a miracle will save us. I get that
saying but I been waiting and praying for my
day of life savings.

Life's too short

I'm staring down at you only to read
for what I have written can live and breathe.
I'm a stranger no more to my words
so be no stranger to feel what you heard.
The time can be a friend of mine, why,
then it can turn against me to my surprise.
The pace speeds up and I tend to get by
when I push more than enough, but why?
The needs to be at my best will arise
as the deeds rest on my shoulders, why?
As I look down still no strangers no feelings of sort
I read to you these words to realize why life's too short.

Masterpiece

With every fine line we find
in time life is defined.
All alone sweet nature creates the wild
on the other side fear in human nature grows wild.
A world of colors come together to ensure the two
a love as colorful as the white and the black are consumed.
A speck from way up high in the baby blue sky
that speck is I from the camouflage eye of a bright peacock
butterfly.
All the texture and all the hue
fall to blend with the white light so this we view.
The very Earthly gestures show true scenery,
the beautiful collection of art known as masterpiece.

Miss

Have you ever felt like your life was misplaced?
Have you never held a light from grace?
I could be in your space so direct
but the wondering stays to become misdirect.
I would be a soul mate sailing so great,
however, the wind sways away to miscalculate.
I should be the one to hold love for you
instead the feeling strays until misconstrue.
I appear to be circling in your head
still unaware if I will see you or be misled.
I know at times we will connect what's a midst
because together we both know what we miss.

My Kingdom

I am standing to the west
there the air fairs the best.
This is where my tension rests,
and my attention is kept. Here I feel
peace lives in each breathe. The sweet
place seems to sweep my feet from under me.
I am no longer standing. The space fills until
my dream of being a King among an Ace is
fulfilled magically. Yes, I am no longer in my
loom of doom instead I am among my friend,
the wind in my Kingdom. I would have never
known that along a winding back road
would behold this scene. I mean if I
were not lost I would have never found
my place to be. This peaceful space,
my Kingdom to breathe.

Naked

I dress myself every day
to address the World in a fashionable way.
My shirt hides some skin
as my pants glides on in.
I cruise along in my big ride
to get to my job to make it right.
My work fulfills me just enough
but my bills pile up and up.
I feel so much stress when I breathe
as I sweat over the mess I bleed.
It's hard to pin point or detect it
but inside I feel emotionally naked.

Observant

A look that took continues
to look the crook that pursues
this stare is for what is fair
when there is more of the unfair.
The blame, a shame, on the servant
the name, defamed, just a servant.
the eyes of help seen the thief
the same eyes that cry a grief.
The jewel shines from the other's pocket
the look was priceless like that locket.
the name was cleared of the good servant
the look for the truth was observant.

Our Hands

A soft delicate touch
to brush all that is too much.
The nails that grows so long
to scratch away all the wrong.
The caring held very gently
to understand with compassion truly.
The lines so unique like Heaven sent
to make an identity with finger prints.
A world of words created with gesture sings
to communicate a language unheard so define.
The love, trust, choices, and plans
all the attention rest within our hands.

Perceived

A thought from a long time ago
it can be changed along a different road.
The reasons it gave you heartache & pain
like the seasons can show beauty all the same.
The younger you are the more the idea hurts
the older you get the thought simply works.
The time seems endless as the clock ticks
the memories forever kept in a box as it ticks.
The life that was together to form one,
picks up the pieces to find the trust in another one.
A thought from the past shown deceit
it can only be seen its truth until perceived.

Plenty

Things go bad as times get sad
so you need a drink but there's an empty glass.
You reach for the wine in a bottle
as you fill it half way it's hard to swallow.
It's even harder to think so you wallow
in your own tears until there's tomorrow.
The next day you feel empty not a single tear
what once filled within you is no longer here.
Things get better with time in this weather
you start to shine and love shows the forever.
You reach for something to drink, so thirsty,
the glass is so full you realize you have plenty.

P.S.: A Hopeless Romantic

Dear Ladies,
I am so crazy
I have looked around
for that special girl to love me.
I am always on the go, go, go.
Well, I am not lazy.
I will wait till I find that someone
that makes me feel amazing.
As long as the sun rises and sets
I will remain careless.

Sincerely Yours,
A Gentleman

P.S.: A Hopeless Romantic

Dear Ladies,
I am so silly
I have took a look beyond
and above me. My soul just
waiting to be set free.
My love just wanting to
see a girl to be true to me.
I will wait till that time
the special someone will
blow my mind with kindness.
As long as the tides rise and fall
I will remain careful.

Sincerely Yours,
A Gentleman

P.S.: A Hopeless Romantic

Raped

All the sweat and all the tears
can make up for all those lost years.
Taken away by most of the pain
making a better place more than a name.
Dusting myself off from the blame
trusting I am well done from the flame.
Picked apart piece by piece
put back together still missing a piece.
Left dead in my tracks then
right ahead and I'm back there again.
I live it up in a blaze of mistake
even if in the end I may feel raped.

Round

From one point to another around
that shape is circling a bound
into a bond our hearts surround
rising to a beat that perfect sound
no matter the pound after a pound
we come together then back round
I found.

Sacrifices

I have a life of hopes and dreams
I have a will of wants and needs.
I give all this away every single day
to empower my kids to show a better way.
I am a father and they come first
after all it is time to teach as they thirst.
I take no moment for granted
no matters the distance from ex love so against it.
I don't have to prove anything at all
that is why I succeed at every wall.
The focus is a single Dad, two girls, the vices
and the giving of my life for those sacrifices.

Saved by the bell

Before I was saved by the bell, I was living
in a hell, a prisoner in a cell. Going
insane feeling all this pain. Thinking,
nothing would be sane and everything
would never be the same, but then I was
saved by the bell. Knocked outside of my
shell. I woke up from my hell, no longer
a prisoner in a cell. Stronger than my
pain, and I can see now things have
changed. And I can accept what is not
the same because I believe how my change
made me. I fell but then I was saved
by the bell. I was touched by an angel.
No longer in a spell, once again seeing a
heaven not just a hell. Not having the
feeling of being alone because I have
found myself. And I will go on and on
knowing that I was saved by the bell.

Shed the fine Thoughts

My time has been for a while 50/50
but my vision in mind profiles 20/20.
I know it takes some time for the way
to show the mistakes a better place.
The rest of the time created the maze
to roam the grounds because Rome took days.
The mind reminds the time lost all around
that the eyes can smile after the frown upside down.
The subconscious is falling for the less is more,
and the conscious is calling for an encore.
The time 50/50, the mind's eye 20/20 brought
the days along those ways to shed the fine thoughts.

The Greatest American Novel

We all write the greatest American novels
as we live, cry, and love consonants and vowels.
The universal truth is hurt so well put into words
the grief passes so fruitful among different worlds.
The design is a negative natural disaster
that was created to find mind over matter.
The matter is the distance of all
as the ladder of resistance did break to fall.
The destination between love and hate aligns
with the stars so positive handwriting a line into lines.
The connection from sin to pen is an idea so novel
as many worlds spin to read The Greatest American Novel.

The path

I follow my reasons all alone
to allow my dreams to be known.
I stare real hard when it's sad
then I share what's beneath when it's bad.
I don't know what the future will hold
but I do know that my will is bold.
I don't please anyone anymore in anyway
I believe in myself that I have a way.
I understand there's jealousy and greed
I comprehend what I want and need.
One might follow the wrong, the sad, and the wrath
but I allow a strong mind and heart to the soul that's the path.

The sport of court

My pulse is racing, my heart is beating at
a fast pace, and beads of sweat pass along my
face. I'm feeling kind of nervous running around
in this place. It is not too fun where I am, no,
it is not basketball camp or a fifty yard dash. Sorry,
this is no true sport instead it is me back in court.
My ex-wife is so out of sorts because year after
year she takes me back to court. I guess she
thinks it is the sport of court. I have to call
my agent that is my lawyer. I have to renew my
contract, that is with my loan officer. I have
to ensue a game plan, that means time off from
my employer. Ready or not here comes the big
game day. No one really can say if they have
won or lost because time after time everything stays
the same, except for the cost. I pray one day
she will see a different way. It is ashamed, well,
until then I really do not welcome to the Hall of
Fame the sport of court.

There-there

My head hurts to think
because my heart returns to the brink.
As my pulse beats in my wrist
my pain remembered my broken fist.
The cold weather brings back the ache
as my thoughts recreate that mistake.
I guess that broken part of me
although healed up still can breathe.
It's up to my emotions that have healed up enough
to remind my feelings in thought to catch up.
I know the present is so clear and the future is ready to share
the past at last I can say there-there.

Through the Sun

Through the sun
I found someone
to lean on, one on one
through the sun.
I discovered everyone
I am not the only one
through the sun.
I believe I am at one
to see less is no less than anyone
through the sun.

Time

If time was a true friend
I would know where to begin
I would know when I am
to stay, to go, how to understand.
If time was a true friend
I would know of no end
I would know then I am
to leave, to show, I understand,
if time was a true friend.

Toward the dawn

It is just so-so right
to feel this wrong.
When losing sight
of how to hold strong.
When choosing might
show a light off and not on.
When confusing at the night
dim lights come along.
When ensuing another light
a new is toward the dawn.

Trust

If you don't have trust
then you don't have a love.
If you don't have love
then you don't have some hugs.
If you don't have hugs
then you don't have the what's up?
If you don't have what's up
then you don't have the most of.
If you don't have most of
then you don't have the above.
If you don't have all the above
then you don't have trust.

Two

I thought the same way as you
I felt the aches and pain too.
My days of hardship did bruise
as your ways of doubt created blues.
My dreams fell apart at the moon
just like your heart broke that noon.
The time went on I was so confused
not knowing anyone else shared my views.
By chance we met to reflect the news
we both connect from what we went through.
A friend to ease my mind of this simple truth
the paths so hard to choose show not one but two.

Way down in that hole

When I was way down in that hole, where no one comes
or goes; I just could not behold or be told which way to
go. There, I never felt so alone. Although suddenly and thankfully
I gave myself a way, then bam! A flash
of light was shown. I stopped digging in that hole.
It is then I finally realized and heard my choices
within me. They spoke word after word to me, I
opened up honestly as my voice was drawn out
of me. Next, I moved along with forgiveness while
covering that hole. Then my days started to show
and tell how, why, and where, I was. I can
say I was way down in that hole of darkness
and the pain was unbearable because I was ashamed
and blamed myself. Although suddenly and thankfully, I gave
myself a way, then bam! A flash
of light showed brighter days. My blame became
my flame, my shame became my fame, my darkness
became my light, my pain became my sight. I
was way down in that hole, but I became so much
more safe and sound as my truth became found
way down in that hole.

Well Traveled Path

The well traveled path can be seen
as a way the faults did lead.
For the errors had to breathe
while the scars, so bad, did bleed.
The going through it at no stop
was showing strength beyond a drop.
From the first step until the leap
what once was so flat became so steep.
The struggles to show a forever together
became the rubbles showing a never ever.
As the way of the faults did lead
it's the well traveled path we believe.

Window of Opportunity

There is disappointment when the door starts closing
and things seem over. Then again, there is always a
window of opportunity showing that keeps us going.
Keep your eyes, those windows open. Do not
leave your mind, your soul, or your heart too
exposed to those opinions that only show more
wrong than truth. Yes, rest assure, when you
follow the facts, your heart of hearts, you can
shine through. Know if things seem unsettled,
open a window, and see to your surprise that
everything will be alright. Please remember, when
there is disappointment approaching once again, behind
the door closing there is a window of opportunity
showing that keeps us going friends.

You have my words

When the faith is broken
and your coinage is unspoken
may a phrase of my poetry
praise our souls to show closely
how we slowly repair and mend
as loving women and men
becoming faithful again within
reading those pearls of wisdom to the known and unknown
stating my friends you have my words.

My Artwork:

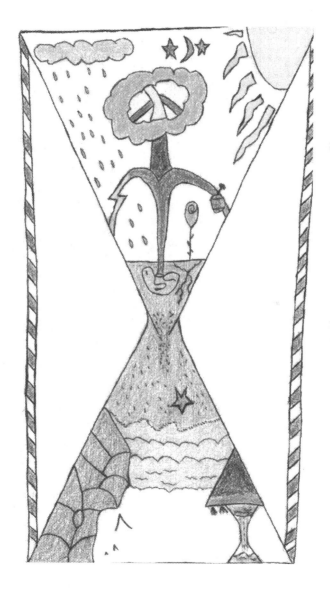

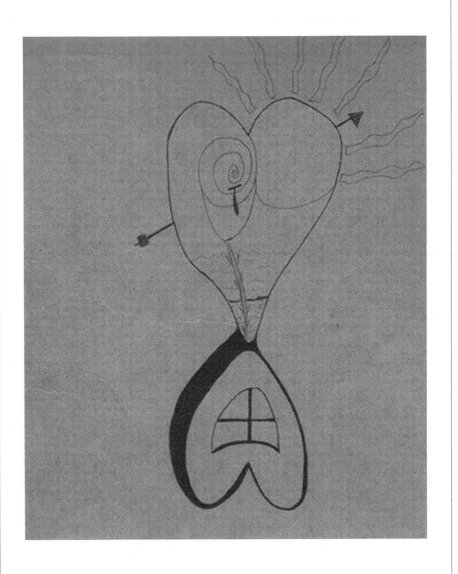

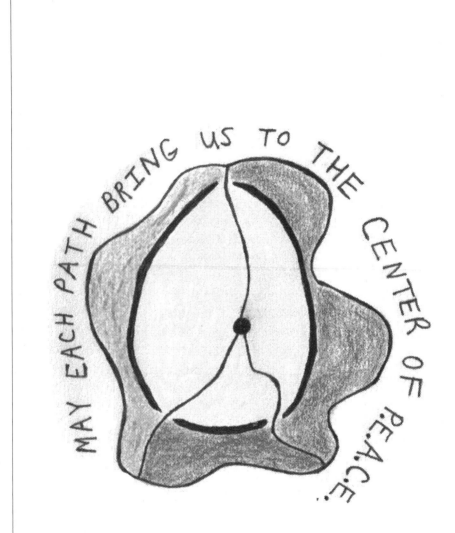

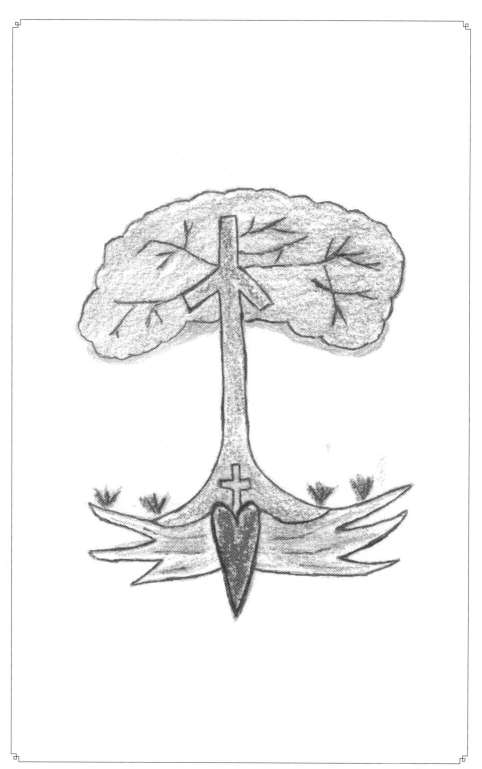

About the Author

I am from a little town called Saint Martinville in Louisiana.
I love spending time with my two daughters;
I enjoy movies, music, and living and learning in the moments
whether good or bad.
I always had a passion for art and in my twelfth grade year of
school picked up on creative writing.
I have a different way of looking at things, and I can see more
clearly if I put the two together, my art and my poetry.
I love words and I hope you love them as much as me. I have
included some of my original artwork too.
In conclusion, the book cover symbolizes everything I wrote from
the end to the new beginning.